THE FLY FISHING GUIDE TO COLORADO'S FLAT TOPS WILDERNESS

Al Marlowe and
Karen Christopherson

WESTWINDS
PRESS®

PRUETT
THE PRUETT SERIES

Library of Congress Cataloging-in-Publication Data
Marlowe, Al, 1938-.
    The fly fishing guide to Colorado's Flat Tops Wilderness / Al Marlowe and Karen Christopherson.
        pages cm. — (The Pruett series)
    Includes bibliographical references and index.
    ISBN 978-0-87108-972-4 (pbk. : alk. paper)
    ISBN: 978-0-87108-995-3 (e-book)
1. Fly fishing—Colorado—Flat Tops Wilderness—Guidebooks. 2. Flat Tops Wilderness (Colo.)—Guidebooks. I. Christopherson, Karen. II. Title.
    SH475.M355 2013
    799.12'4—dc23
                        2013022379

Design by Vicki Knapton

Published by WestWinds Press®
An imprint of

GRAPHIC ARTS
BOOKS®

P.O. Box 56118
Portland, Oregon 97238-6118
(503) 254-5591
www.graphicartsbooks.com

CONTENTS

Introduction

The Flat Tops Plateau is located in west-central Colorado. It is bounded on the south by Interstate 70 through Glenwood Canyon, and on the west by State Highway 13. It lies south of US Highway 40, and State Highway 131 provides access from the east.

Shortly after the beginning of the twentieth century, the US Forest Service planned to develop the shores of Trappers Lake for summer homes. Arthur Carhart, an architect working for the Forest Service at the time, was assigned to lay out lots around the lake. When he observed the beauty of the area, Carhart believed that the land should be preserved. It was through his influence that development plans were abandoned. Carhart's efforts in preserving the land eventually led to passage in 1964 of the Wilderness Act.

This high plateau is covered with numerous lakes and streams. The waters are home to native cutthroats, and nonindigenous species have been stocked, including brook, brown, rainbow, and lake trout. Some of the lakes are shallow and winterkill. The lakes included in this guide are those that normally have fish. Many of the Flat Tops' lakes are unnamed, and little information is available for them. This doesn't mean they are always barren. Anglers should talk with biologists, guides, and lodge managers for information on not-so-well-known fishing holes.

When using this guide be aware that some road names appear different on some maps and from the way they are listed in this guide. A few roads have been re-designated and a few road signs might show those names. The current *National Geographic Trails Illustrated* maps annotate both route numbers and the recent names given to avoid confusion.

NOTE FOR GPS USERS

Coordinates listed in the next section are Lat/Lon and based on US Geological Survey topographic maps. The datum used is North American Datum 1927 (NAD 27). To use with your GPS unit, set it to the above datum and Lat/Lon coordinates. Next enter coordinates as listed. If you will be using maps with a different datum, change it in the GPS navigation setup after entering coordinates. If a different coordinate system (UTM, MGRS, and others) will be used, this should also be changed in the setup after the coordinates are entered. They will then be correct for use with your GPS unit and map.

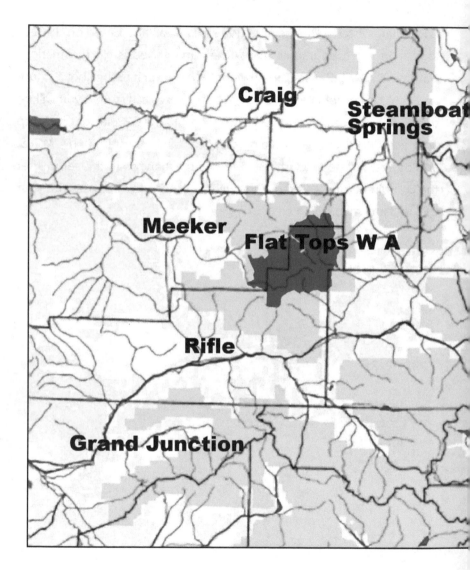

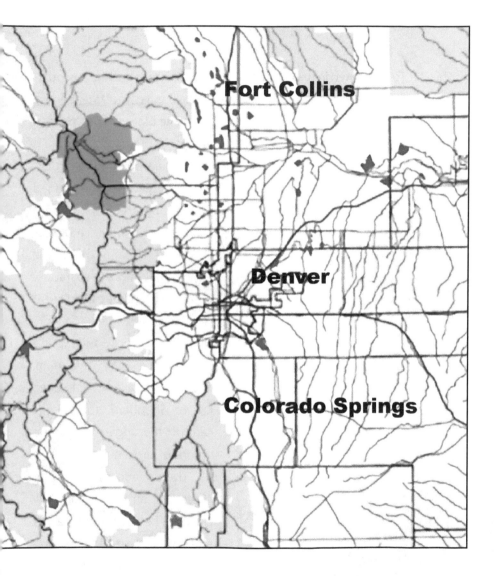

Fort Collins

Denver

Colorado Springs

1

FISHING THE FLAT TOPS

The Flat Tops, located in west-central Colorado, is a place unlike any other mountain range in the state. There are no tall spires, no fourteeners. Rather, it is a high plateau, appearing as a massive block of rock pushed upward by some giant's hand, and planed level.

On its surface, covering several hundred square miles, long extinct volcanic craters are filled with water. In other places, glaciers have gouged deep valleys and plowed debris into ridges, damming streams.

Because of its location, the Flat Tops collects an abundance of precipitation. Water, collected by lakes and drained by streams, makes the region an angler's paradise.

The Colorado River cutthroat is the native trout of Colorado's West Slope. Trappers Lake has a reproducing population.

Creeks with names like Derby, Grizzly, Sweetwater, Canyon, Doe, Fawn, Buck, and Spring pop up all over the map. There's Star Lake, Wall, Keener, Oyster, Shepherd, and others, causing the angler to conjure visions of large, hungry trout.

There's something for anglers of all persuasions. Fly casters have a choice of streams, from small creeks and beaver ponds to rivers hiding fish of surprising proportions. Lakes and ponds beckon to the spinner fisherman. Some have big surprises. If you should try the Mandall Lakes, hang on to your rod. That submerged log you thought you snagged just might be a 10-pound mackinaw.

So where should one begin in a quest for angling adventure in this most magnificent wilderness? For starters, when traveling on Interstate 70, get off at Dotsero and follow the Colorado River upstream for a couple of miles to Deep Creek. The creek runs fast as it plunges and wends its way to the Colorado. For the first mile along the gravel road, the water is private. In another mile, the road departs the creek. It's a small stream in a half-mile-deep canyon, but in the dozen miles below Deep Lake, it's reported to have brooks, rainbows, and few fishermen.

The rough gravel path continues on another 37 miles before ending beside the South Fork of the White River. On the way along the Coffee Pot Road, Deep Lake will tempt the angler to stop off early. Being an extinct volcanic crater, the lake lives up to its name. Its waters hold brook trout and mackinaws. In 1949, a state record mac was taken here— 42 inches long and 36 pounds. The record held until 2007 when a larger mac was taken in Stagecoach Reservoir, just east of the Flat Tops and on the Yampa River drainage.

After another 8 miles, you'll come to The Meadows. The trailhead parking lot gives access to the upper part of the South Fork. It's a small stream, having mostly brook trout. Except in late summer, anglers will find few rising fish, but drifting a No. 12 or 14 Humpy will attract strikes from ravenous trout.

Downstream, the South Fork is larger and faster as it flows toward the South Fork Campground. In between, there's more than a dozen miles of wilderness water. The cutthroats and rainbows are bigger than the brookies found upstream, but they're just as impatient to take a fly.

Along the north side of the Flat Tops, go east out of Meeker on Rio Blanco County Road 8. At Buford, the South and North forks blend their waters. Continuing east from Buford takes you along the North Fork of the White. Being easier to reach, it gets fished more than the South. By carefully studying your White River National Forest map, though, you'll be able to find a few out-of-the-way stretches of public water that hold brookies, browns, rainbows, and cutthroats, all eager to take your fly.

Continuing upstream along the North Fork takes you to Trappers, the best-known lake on the Flat Tops, home to naturally reproducing cutthroat trout. A mile to the east sits Little Trappers. This 30-acre lake can be easily fished from shore for 12-inch cutts.

Then there are places like Mirror Lake, a few miles north of Trappers. Hordes of brookies can be seen in the lake's clear water as they scour the surface in search of edibles. With a seemingly unlimited supply of fish, any method goes here. This is an ideal place to introduce a friend to fly fishing. Which fly? Whatever you want to tie on, although a No. 12 Rio Grande King will be voraciously attacked by the little monsters.

County Road 8 continues east to Ripple Creek Pass. A half mile west of the summit, a trail points north to Pagoda Peak. A mile southwest of the peak lies Pagoda Lake, a small tree-lined lake holding 12-inch brookies eager to take a fly or spinner. By late June, the snow will be gone. The 4-mile walk is easy, making this a pleasant overnighter for backpackers.

All of the lakes and streams mentioned so far are easily accessed by vehicle or a short walk. The ambitious angler, who savors the wilderness experience as much as the fishing, will want to load up a backpack or packhorse and head for the back country. A study of the topographic maps of the Flat Tops reveals many high country lakes. Many are shallow, fishless potholes, scoured by glaciers. Others winterkill periodically. Quite a few lakes, though, are consistent producers.

Most of the lakes are stocked with cutthroats, though brook trout are plentiful and a few have rainbows and mackinaws. In the majority, expect to find fish of 8 to 12 inches, a perfect size for the skillet. A few hold cutts averaging close to 16 inches.

Since most streams on the plateau are headwaters, often brush-lined, fishing them can be both challenging and rewarding. Most creeks will be productive during spawning periods when fish run up inlet streams to make more fish.

A few miles east of Buford, detour south to Marvine Creek. It's small, as are many of its fish—but not all. Lurking in some of the clear, deep pools, sulking forms of 12-inch cutts and rainbows will be seen by anglers who carefully approach the water.

At the end of County Road 12, Trail 1823 follows Marvine Creek for 6 miles to the two Marvine Lakes. The upper has brook trout. Cutthroats and brookies are taken in the lower. Both lakes have adequate open shoreline for a backcast. The stream below the lower lake is good for small brookies.

Between Ripple Creek Pass (on the north side of the Flat Tops) and Stillwater Reservoir (10 miles south) lie a number of lakes worth casting a fly into. All require a hike or horse ride of at least 5 miles. If you have llamas or packhorses available, take your belly boat. Shorelines on these moraine-dammed lakes are often overgrown with lodgepoles and spruce trees, making casting a challenge. A float tube will get you away from these obstacles.

Okay, so now that we have some ideas of places to fish, what do we use? In some cases, method is determined by regulation. In Trappers Lake, it's flies and lures only. And since many of the fish caught must be returned because of size restrictions, it won't hurt to pinch down the barbs on flies and avoid the use of treble hooks on lures.

Fly casters have the greatest choice, especially those who are also tiers. Brook trout in lakes are attracted to brightly colored patterns, like a Royal Coachman streamer in sizes 6 to 12. Spruce Fly streamers should

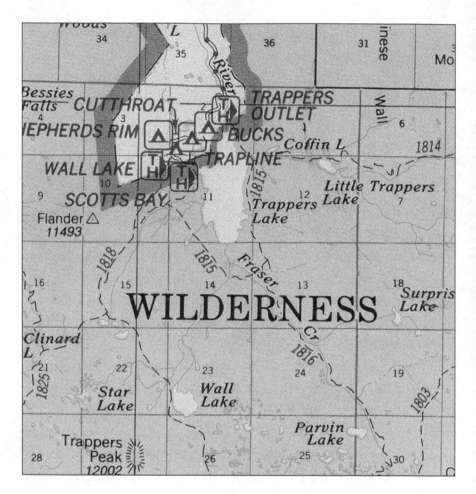

Trappers is the largest natural lake in the Flat Tops Wilderness.

also work. Use a sinking line to get the fly down deep, and retrieve it with short twitches. Woolly Buggers in green, black, or brown are good to troll from a belly boat. Use a sinking line here, too.

Beginning as early as June, but usually occurring in July, the *Callibaetis* hatch gets underway. This is a small, dark mayfly that trout ravenously devour. In some lakes, like Trappers for example, the cutthroats have become somewhat educated. At times they will take only a well-presented imitation. A good pattern for the hatch is a No. 16 Parachute Adams. It can be hard to go wrong with a Humpy or an Elk Hair Caddis. Fish these in a size that approximates the naturals on the water. Be sure to include patterns like the Adams in your fly box, especially in small sizes. Lake fish seem to go for gray.

Sometimes those rising fish aren't taking adult insects. When that's the case, switch to a Hare's Ear nymph in an appropriate size and color: tan, brown, or olive. If you tie your own, make the wing case with Crystal Hair or Crystal Flash to better imitate an emerging insect, and fish it in the surface film.

Be sure to include patterns imitating other aquatic life forms. Leeches and scuds are some of the more common trout foods other than insects. Colors for Woolly Buggers should include purple, brown, and green. The most common colors for scuds are green and gray. Don't forget to include terrestrials in your fly box. Grasshoppers, ants, and beetles will take fish at various times, especially in late summer.

Although bait is legal in all but a few waters, because of conditions in the Flat Tops, it's better to avoid using it. One condition is the restrictive limits in place since 1998 of two fish taken from a stream, or four fish from a lake. Parks and Wildlife research has shown that mortality is highest for fish taken with bait. Trout caught on flies, if carefully handled and released, experience mortality of 4 percent or less, much smaller than for fish taken on bait or lures.

Because of whirling disease, in recent years, fewer trout have been available for stocking in wilderness areas, including the Flat Tops. Some smaller lakes may hold only one or two hundred fish. Trout, particularly the cutthroats, do not spawn successfully in many waters. This means that each fish taken may not be replaced for several years, if at all. Considering the impact of whirling disease on hatchery fish to stock, the higher mortality when using bait, and that if each angler to fish a remote lake

Small streams often hold big surprises.

were to keep a limit of four, it's clear that some lakes could be barren in a short time. Although catch-and-release angling isn't a panacea, the reduced mortality when fishing with flies will make the resource go further. Anglers who enjoy a meal of fresh trout would do well to keep only what will be eaten.

Fishing the Flat Tops lakes usually means getting there early. Ice-out is the ideal time. Unfortunately, many of the lakes will be difficult to reach— it may require skis or snowshoes. The effort has its rewards, though; fewer people, more fish. It also has bigger fish.

Later in the season, when the snows have melted, the lakes will be most productive early and late in the day. As the sun creeps higher, the fish will retreat to deeper water, making them hard to reach from shore. A belly boat will pay off then.

Stream fishermen have just the opposite situation presented them. Both forks of the White River are at their peak flows early. But by mid-July, they're often running clear. Fly fishing begins to peak as the water flow declines. Warm, sunny days bring out hordes of bugs, attracting fish. Mid-morning to late afternoon seems to be the most productive time to be on the water.

With the Flat Tops' many streams and lakes, accessible by nearly 400 miles of trails, an angler would be hard-pressed to fish every lake and stream in a summer. But why try? Study your White River National Forest map, along with the topos. Pick out a few spots to visit. But save one special place for next season, because you will be compelled to return.

Now that you're all fired up to fish the Flat Tops, you want to know how to get there, right? Interstate 70 takes you along the south flank of the plateau and connects with state and county roads on the east and west. At Wolcott, at Milepost 157, State Highway 131 heads north to Steamboat Springs. Jumping-off places at Yampa, Phippsburg, and Oak Creek give access to the east side of the wilderness. Get off the Interstate in Dotsero at Milepost 133, and follow Eagle County 301 to reach the Coffee Pot Road, Sweetwater Lake area, and Derby Mesa.

West of Glenwood Springs, at Rifle, head north 41 miles on State Highway 13 to Meeker. At Meeker, Rio Blanco County Road 8 follows the White River east, crosses Ripple Creek Pass, and eventually arrives at Yampa. County Road 8 connects with other county and Forest Service roads that lead to trailheads.

The Flat Tops is a great place for extended angling trips. Forest Service campgrounds are plentiful. You will find those around Trappers Lake usually busy, though. Primitive camping is permitted in most areas, except along some of the busier roads.

For those who wish to rough it in comfort, there are a several lodges serving the area. See the appendix for a listing of services.

Over the years, the lakes in the Flat Tops have been stocked with brook, brown, cutthroat, and rainbow trout, and a few lakes received mackinaw (lake) trout. Brook trout are able to spawn successfully in most lakes, and are also difficult to eradicate once a population is established. Mackinaw trout also successfully spawn in lakes, and do well in deep lakes. When feed conditions are right, they typically live much longer than other trout. Brown, cutthroat, and rainbow trout generally require an inlet or outlet stream to spawn. Because not all lakes in the Flat Tops have ideal stream habitat, maintaining populations of these three depends largely on stocking.

Species data for lakes was acquired from a number of sources, and stocking dates are included where they are available from Colorado Parks and Wildlife. In general, if a lake is reported to have had brook trout in the past, it's likely they still live in there. Cutthroat and rainbow trout typically need to be stocked every few years to maintain catchable numbers. Lakes listed that show the last stocking occurring five or more years in the past probably have few, if any, cutthroats or rainbows left. Keep this in mind when planning a trip to any lake listed in this guide.

Two fires that burned large areas during 2002 had an impact on a few lakes. Some lakes were eliminated as fisheries, at least over the next few years. Waters that were severely affected by the Big Fish and Lost Lakes Fires are noted in the descriptions.

2

RIO BLANCO COUNTY

County Road 8

Rio Blanco CR 8 is the primary road between Meeker and Yampa. At the White River National Forest boundary east of Buford, it becomes FR 8. At the summit of Ripple Creek Pass, it changes to FR 16, the White River/ Routt NF boundary. The designation changes again at the Routt County line, where it becomes CR 132. Continuing on the same road for 3.5 miles, it joins Routt CR 17, which goes to Yampa.

Anglers try to tempt a trout from the North Fork of the White River.

White River

The Oak Ridge State Wildlife Area east of Meeker gives access to the White River in several places along CR 8. The first is the Sleepy Cat Ponds, 16 miles east of Meeker. Another mile east is the Sleepy Cat Fishing Easement at the Sleepy Cat Guest Ranch on the south side of the highway. At 18 miles, the river is open to angling east to the Bel Aire Unit, which is the site of a former fish hatchery. Public access to the river east of Meeker is marked with Colorado Parks and Wildlife (CPW) signs.

The river has brook, brown, cutthroat, and rainbow trout, and whitefish.

LAKE AVERY (BIG BEAVER RESERVOIR)

Elevation: 6,985 ft.   **39° 59' 11.84" N**   **107° 38' 33.74" W**

» 264 acres; 76 feet deep; cutthroat and rainbow trout.
» Lake Avery, 20 miles east of Meeker on CR 8, was built by Colorado Parks and Wildlife for recreation. There are campgrounds at the inlet and near the west end of the dam. Both have limited facilities and spaces. No drinking water. The lake has good feed conditions that promote fast growth of the fish, but fishing results are

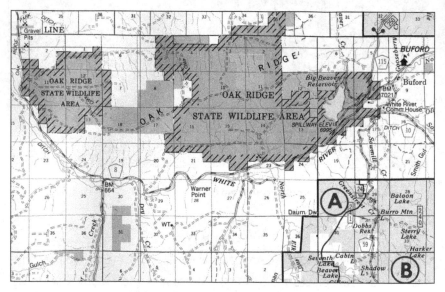

Big Beaver Reservoir

variable. As is true of most high lakes, the best angling comes after ice-out and in the spring.

» One mile west of Buford, an access road heads north to Lake Avery.
» A mile south of Buford, take CR 59, which becomes FR 245. It's the Buford-New Castle road. At Hiner Spring, FR 601, a 4-wheel-drive road gives access to several lakes.

MEADOW CREEK LAKE

Elevation: 9,550 ft.   **39° 48′ 48.60″ N**   **107° 26′ 12.46″ W**

» Brook and possibly rainbow trout.
» At Hiner Spring, go 2 miles east on FR 601, then 2 miles south on FR 823 to the lake and Meadow Lake Campground.

CLIFF LAKES

Elevation: 9,660 ft.   **39° 50′ 22.91″ N**   **107° 32′ 36.81″ W**

» 3 acres; 7 feet deep; brook and rainbow trout.
» At Hiner Spring, go 2 miles east on FR 601 to Cliff Lake Trailhead, then 0.5 mile on a 4-wheel-drive road to the lakes.
» Forest Road 601 connects with FR 640 to access the Blair Lake Trail. All roads in this area are rough and 4-wheel drive is highly recommended.
» The following lakes are also accessed from FR 640. See the directions to Heart Lake.

MAHAFFEY LAKE

Elevation: 9,783 ft.   **39° 50′ 30.58″ N**   **107° 26′ 16.52″ W**

» 10 acres; 61 feet deep; rainbow trout.

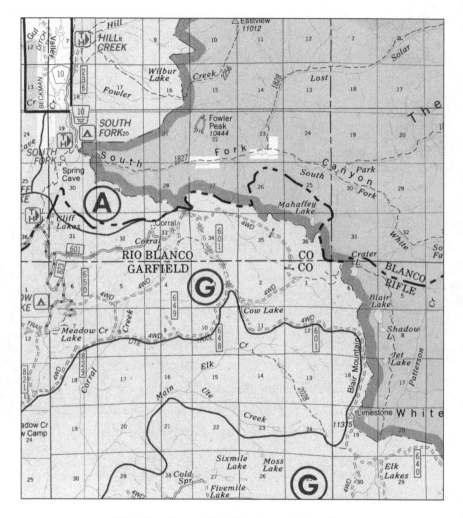

Mahaffey, Crater, Blair, Shadow, and Jet Lakes

» At Hiner Spring, take FR 601 8 miles to FR 647, then 3 miles to Crater Lake Trailhead. No trail, so go cross-country down a very steep slope to the lake.

CRATER LAKE

Elevation: 10,263 ft.   **39° 57′ 57.66″ N**   **107° 33′ 03.48″ W**

» 16 acres; 100 feet deep; brook trout.
» At Hiner Spring, take FR 601 8 miles to FR 647, then 3 miles to Crater Lake Trailhead. Take Blair Lake Trail 2098 1 mile east, down a steep slope to Crater Lake.

BLAIR LAKE

Elevation: 10,466 ft.   **39° 48′ 43.64″ N**   **107° 24′ 36.92″ W**

» 28 acres; 100 feet deep; brook, cutthroat, and rainbow trout. Last stocking was 1994.
» At Hiner Spring, take FR 601 8 miles to FR 647, then 3 miles to Crater Lake Trailhead. Take Blair Lake Trail 2098 east, then down a steep slope 2 miles to lake. The lake is 0.25 mile west of the trail.

SHADOW LAKE

Elevation: 10,456 ft.   **39° 48′ 24.17″ N**   **107° 24′ 32.29″ W**

» 6 acres; 20 feet deep; rainbow trout.
» At Hiner Spring, take FR 601 8 miles to FR 647, then 3 miles to Crater Lake Trailhead. Take Blair Lake Trail 2098 east, then down a steep slope 2.5 miles to lake. The lake is 0.25 mile west of the trail.

JET LAKE

Elevation: 10,335 ft.	39° 47′ 53.66″ N	107° 24′ 30.07″ W

» 8 acres; 60 feet deep; brook trout, rainbow trout (last stocked in 1994), and cutthroats (stocked in 1992).

» At Hiner Spring, take FR 601 8 miles to FR 647, then 3 miles to Crater Lake Trailhead. Take Blair Lake Trail 2098 east, then down a steep slope 4 miles to lake.

» An easier alternate route to Jet, Shadow, and Blair Lakes is possible. At Hiner Spring, take FR 601 13 miles to FR 640, then 0.5 mile to Patterson Creek Trailhead. Blair Lake Trail 2098 heads north 2 miles to Jet Lake.

County Road 10 : South Fork of the White River

At Buford, the South and North Fork merge to form the White River. South of Buford, the Oak Ridge State Wildlife Area gives public access to the last mile of the South Fork. The river is large and not easy to cross in most places.

CR 10, a mile south of Buford, runs parallel to the river 9 miles to the South Fork Campground, the next public access. The South Fork gets lots of pressure near the campground, but there are rainbow trout and whitefish.

Follow Trail 1827 upstream along the river. Good dry fly fishing for cutthroat and rainbow trout. Beginning 4 miles from the trailhead, two half-mile sections of the river run through private holdings inside the wilderness and these stretches may be posted.

BAILEY LAKE

Elevation: 8,790 ft.   **39° 57′ 57.66″ N**   **107° 33′ 03.48″ W**

» 5 acres; brook and rainbow trout reported in the past, but no recent stocking.

» On CR 10 2 miles south from Buford, park at the trailhead for Trail 1825; 4 miles to the lake.

SWEDE LAKE

Elevation: 8,880 ft.   **39° 58′ 01.25″ N**   **107° 33′ 3.48″ W**

» 4 acres; 6 feet deep; brook and rainbow trout reported in the past, but no recent stocking.

» On CR 10 2 miles south from Buford, park at the trailhead for Trail 1825; 4.5 miles to the lake.

» From Swede Lake, the trail heads east to the plateau and continues across the Flat Tops to the Wall Lake Trail (Trail 1818). There are countless lakes along the way, including Clam, Papoose, Oyster, Twin, Clinard, and Star Lakes, and many unnamed waters. For most, little or no data is available. Some of the lodges maintain the lakes for their clients. If a lake or creek appears to have fish, it's best to check it out with a rod and fly.

PELTIER LAKE

Elevation: 8,892 ft.   **39° 55′ 39.80″ N**   **107° 31′ 32.13″ W**

» 13 acres; 7 feet deep; brook trout reported in the past. CPW has no record of stocking.

» Take CR 10 9 miles to the Hill Creek Trailhead. Trail 1826 heads north 3 miles to the lake. The shoreline is open.

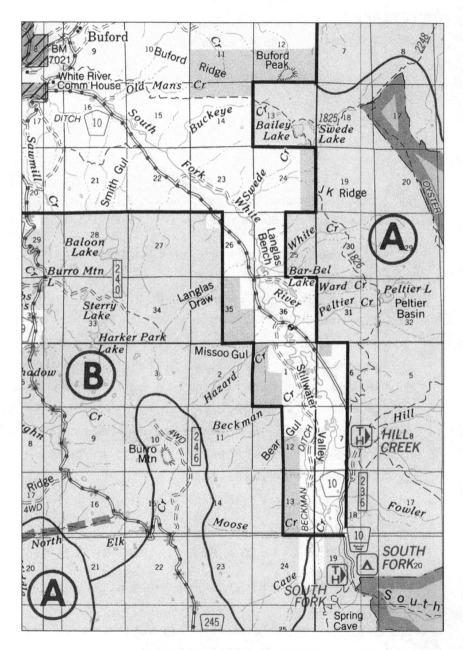

Bailey, Swede, and Peltier Lakes

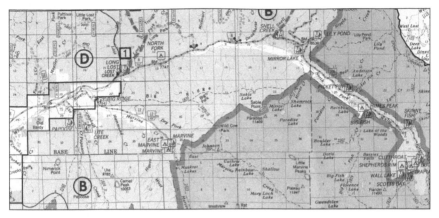

North Fork of the White River

North Fork of the White River

Along CR 8 west of FR 205, nearly 3 miles of the river is open on White River National Forest land. Park along the road near the Snell Creek Trailhead. The White can be fished downstream to the first fence that marks the Rio Blanco Ranch, and upstream for a couple of miles. Fly fishing is good for brook, brown, cutthroat, and rainbow trout. The current is fast in most sections and difficult to wade at flows above 200 cubic feet per second (cfs).

» A 3.5-mile section runs through national forest in the area of the North Fork Campground. All methods are legal, but fly fishing is usually the most productive method.

Cutthroats like this one await anglers in Flat Tops waters.

Rio Blanco : County Road 12

CR 12 gives access to the Ute Creek Trailhead and all forks of Marvine Creek. The road leaves CR 8 6 miles east of Buford. It is also accessed 8 miles east of Buford.

East Fork Marvine Creek

The East Fork is a small, brushy stream with a high gradient. It's mostly pocket water, and difficult to fish.

The following lakes are accessed from CR 12 and FR 12. Park at the Marvine Trailhead and take Trail 1822.

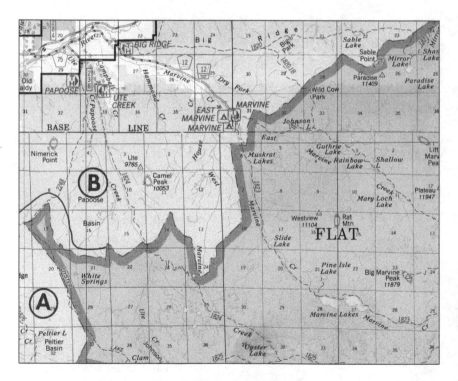

Marvine Lakes

JOHNSON LAKE

Elevation: 8,980 ft.   **40° 00′ 16.56″ N**   **107° 23′ 22.06″ W**

- » 3 acres; 4 feet deep; rainbow trout (no stocking in recent years).
- » It's a murky lake with mainly small fish, although it's reported that an occasional large rainbow is taken.
- » Access is 2 miles from the Marvine Trailhead.

GUTHRIE LAKES

Elevation: 9,270 ft.   **39° 59′ 47.74″ N**   **107° 22′ 13.77″ W**

- » 2 acres; 4 and 5 feet deep; brook and cutthroat trout reported in the past, but CPW has no record of stocking.
- » The lakes are 3.5 miles from Marvine Trailhead and a short distance south of the trail.

RAINBOW LAKE

Elevation: 9,520 ft.   **39° 59′ 40.46″ N**   **107° 21′ 39.72″ W**

- » 2 acres; 8 feet deep.
- » Brook and cutthroat stocked in 1996, and rainbow trout stocked in 1994.
- » The lake is 4 miles from the Marvine Trailhead.

SHALLOW LAKE

Elevation: 9,560 ft.   **39° 59′ 30.42″ N**   **107° 21′ 25.26″ W**

- » 1 acre; cutthroat and rainbow trout.
- » It is beside the trail 5 miles from the Marvine Trailhead.

MARY LOCH LAKE

Elevation: 9,800 ft.   **39° 58' 45.34" N**   **107° 20' 47.99" W**

» 3 acres; 11 feet deep.
» Cutthroat and rainbow trout reported in the past, but no recent stocking has occurred.
» Located 6 miles from the Marvine Trailhead. The lake is a short distance from the trail and surrounded by heavy timber.

Marvine Creek

The creek has about 3 miles of public access inside the forest boundary along FR 12. It's small and brushy with a high gradient. It has brook, cutthroat, and rainbow trout, and whitefish are reported. Several unmarked roads give access to the stream south of the forest boundary.

Inside the wilderness, the stream is smaller with a few ponds between the boundary and Lower Marvine Lake. Immediately below the lower lake, the stream is good for a few larger fish.

The following lakes are accessed from CR 12 and FR 12. Park at the Marvine Trailhead and take Trail 1823.

SLIDE LAKE

Elevation: 8,670 ft.   **39° 57' 46.00" N**   **107° 24' 36.70" W**

» 12 acres; 6 feet deep.
» Brook, cutthroat, and rainbow trout may have been stocked in past years, but presently mostly small brook trout.
» Location is 3 miles from the Marvine Trailhead.

PINE ISLE LAKE

Elevation: 9,240 ft.   39° 57′ 00.54″ N   107° 23′ 00.28″ W

- » 7 acres; 33 feet deep; cutthroat trout stocked in 2001.
- » Fishing is best at ice-out, but this usually means getting there on skis or snowshoes.
- » Access is 6 miles from the trailhead, then take an unmarked trail 0.5 mile north to the lake.

RUBY LAKE

Elevation: 9,110 ft.   39° 57′ 09.60″ N   107° 23′ 25.83″ W

- » 1 acre; cutthroat and rainbow trout.
- » Ruby Lake is located 0.25 mile northwest of Pine Isle Lake. No trail and the lake is not named on USGS, USFS, or *Trails Illustrated* maps.

LOWER MARVINE LAKE

Elevation: 9,308 ft.   39° 56′ 33.94″ N   107° 23′ 01.09″ W

- » 65 acres, 57 feet deep; brook and cutthroat trout.
- » It is 6 miles from the Marvine Trailhead along the west side of the trail.

UPPER MARVINE LAKE

Elevation: 9,317 ft.   39° 56′ 32.34″ N   107° 22′ 20.93″ W

- » 88 acres, 59 feet deep; brook and cutthroat trout.
- » Upper Marvine sits 7 miles from the Marvine Trailhead along the west side of the trail.

Forest Road 205:
North Fork of the White River, Upper Section

The North Fork heads at Trappers Lake. It's closed to fishing for a short distance that's marked below the lake. Once it comes near FR 205, it's open for angling to the Rio Blanco Ranch near Himes Peak Campground. The ranch is well posted, so it isn't a problem to find the closed stretches.

The section across the road from Trappers Lake Lodge is heavily fished, but it's still good for cutthroat and rainbow trout averaging 7 to 10 inches. There are no restrictions on method, but it's good fly fishing water for anglers at all levels of experience.

The next place to fish is the run near the Skinny Fish Trailhead. It's primarily pocket water—fast currents with a few deeper holes.

SHAMROCK LAKE

Elevation: 9,820 ft.	40° 02' 5.57" N	107° 20' 1.72" W

- » 2 acres; 14 feet deep; brook trout.
- » From FR 205, park at Mirror Lake Trailhead. Go 3 miles on Trail 1821.

MIRROR LAKE

Elevation: 10,010 ft.	40° 01' 42.86" N	107° 20' 11.71" W

- » 17 acres; 70 feet deep; brook trout.
- » From FR 205, park at Mirror Lake Trailhead. Go 4 miles on Trail 1821.

SABLE LAKE

Elevation: 9,882 ft.	40° 02' 29.75" N	107° 02' 53.94" W

- » 7 acres; 20 feet deep; cutthroat trout stocked in 2001.
- » From FR 205, park at Mirror Lake Trailhead. Go 3 miles on Trail 1821,

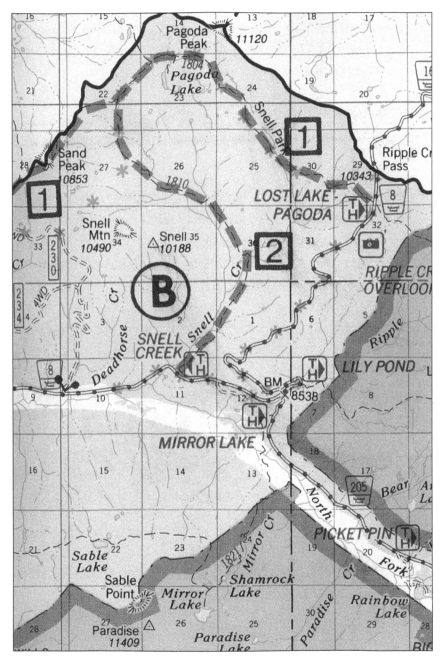

Shamrock, Mirror, Sable, and Pagoda Lakes

a short distance past Shamrock Lake, and 3 miles on Trail 1820 to Sable Lake. You can also get there from CR 12. Park at Big Ridge Trailhead. On Trail 1820, it's 7 miles to lake.

ANDERSON LAKE (RESERVOIR)

Elevation: 9,340 ft.   **39° 02′ 47.66″ N**   **107° 17′ 9.88″ W**

» 7 acres; 38 feet deep.
» Brook trout fishing is good, but sometimes winterkills. There's usually enough fish survive to repopulate the lake. Feed conditions permit brook trout to grow up to 14 inches.
» From Picket Pin Trailhead on FR 205, take the left trail 1.5 miles to the lake.

Anderson Lake is a good lake to hook into a spunky brook trout.

Big Fish Creek

The stream joins the North Fork near Himes Peak campground, and is openfor fishing inside the forest boundary.

Follow Trail 1819 across the Rio Blanco Ranch to the national forest.

BIG FISH LAKE

Elevation: 9,388 ft.   **39° 59' 19.86" N**   **107° 17' 16.87" W**

» 20 acres; 20 feet deep; brook, cutthroat, and rainbow trout.
» The best fishing is at ice-out, but it usually requires the use of skis or snowshoes to get there.
» Take FR 205 south 5 miles to Himes Peak Campground parking lot. Go 4 miles west on Trail 1819 to the lake.

BOULDER LAKE

Elevation: 9,770 ft.   **40° 00' 27.39" N**   **107° 18' 00.91" W**

» 4 acres; 6 feet deep; cutthroat trout stocked in 2001, but the Big Fish Fire of 2002 may have left the lake barren.
» Take FR 205 south 5 miles to Himes Peak Campground parking lot. Go 2 miles west on Trail 1819 to Trail 2262 (40° 00' 46.44" N, 107° 16' 45.97" W), and then 2 miles to Boulder Lake.

DORIS LAKE

Elevation: 10,050 ft.   **40° 00' 12.85" N**   **107° 17' 51.93" W**

» 6 acres; 20 feet deep.
» No information.

Lake of the Woods, Skinny Fish, and McGinnis Lakes

» Take FR 205 south 5 miles to Himes Peak Campground parking lot. Go 2 miles west on Trail 1819 to Trail 2262, 2 miles to Boulder Lake, then cross-country 0.5 mile south to Doris Lake.

GWENDOLEN (GWENDOLYN) LAKE

Elevation: 9,750 ft.   **39° 58′ 26.04″ N**   **107° 17′ 41.63″ W**

» 4 acres; 8 feet deep; barren until cutthroat trout were stocked in 2002.
» Take FR 205 south 5 miles to Himes Peak Campground parking lot. Go 4 miles west on Trail 1819 to Big Fish Lake, then follow the creek upstream 1.5 miles to Gwendolen.

SKINNY FISH LAKE

Elevation: 10,192 ft.   **40° 01′ 58.33″ N**   **107° 12′ 45.58″ W**

» 20 acres; 9 feet deep; brook and cutthroat stocked in 1994, and rainbow trout stocked last in 1990. Spawning is possibly successful in the inlet stream. The lake's name is not an indication of the trout's condition.

» The stream between Upper Skinny Fish and the lower lake is good, as well as the upper lake.

» Park at trailhead 8 miles from CR 8 on FR 205. Take Trail 1813 3 miles to Skinny Fish.

LAKE OF THE WOODS

Elevation: 9,010 ft.	40° 01' 0.37" N	107° 15' 6.77" W

» 8 acres; 7 feet deep; brook trout.

» The Big Fish Fire of 2002 thoroughly burned the area, but brookies were able to recover. A few will exceed 12 inches in length. Short hike makes it a good float-tube lake.

» Park on FR 205, 7 miles from CR 8. Trailhead (40° 01' 05.27" N, 107° 14' 52.96" W) is unmarked. It's 0.25 mile on an easy trail to the lake.

After the 2002 fire, Lake of the Woods is now easily seen from the road.

MCGINNIS LAKE

Elevation: 10,158 ft.	40° 01' 47.52" N	107° 12' 21.64" W

» 23 acres; 14 feet deep; brook, cutthroat stocked in 1994, and rainbow trout stocked in 1991.

» Park at trailhead 8 miles from CR 8 on FR 205. Take Trail 1813 2 miles to unmarked right fork in the trail (40° 01' 46.41" N, 107° 12' 52.98" W); less than 1 mile from the junction to the lake.

Forest Road 209

Not only is Trappers Lake one of the better known landmarks on the Flat Tops, it is also the largest natural body of water in the wilderness. Trappers was created when a wall of ice piled rubble across the north end of the basin, forming a natural dam.

Trappers has long been famous for its nearly pure strain of Colorado River cutthroat trout. In spite of the pressure it receives, it's still a good fishery. This is due in part to special regulations for the lake. The use of bait is prohibited. Anglers are restricted to using flies or lures only, and all fish longer than 10 inches must be released unharmed. Certain areas of the lake, such as inlet streams and the outlet, are off-limits to anglers. This protects the breeding size fish.

In the spring, the cutthroats make spawning runs up the inlet streams around the lake. Colorado Parks and Wildlife biologists net the fish as they try to spawn, to collect the eggs for hatchery operations. The cabins on the east shore are used by CPW personnel during this operation. The

Trappers Lake as seen from the Scotts Bay Trailhead. Notice the burned trees on the east shore of the water.

The North Fork of the White River originates at the outlet of Trappers Lake. Even though the stream is beside the road, fishing can be surprisingly good for small cutts and brookies.

Colorado River cutthroat is considered a threatened species, and rearing in the Division's hatcheries is one way the species is being protected.

Because Trappers is within the wilderness, the use of motorized equipment is prohibited. This doesn't mean you can't get out on the lake. Hand-propelled boats are allowed, as are belly boats. Trappers Lake Lodge rents rowboats and canoes, which are kept on the lake.

To help preserve the wilderness environment around the lake, camping is prohibited within 0.25 mile of the shoreline. However, campgrounds are provided on the northwest side of Trappers Lake, and are accessible by cars, trailers, and RVs.

TRAPPER'S LAKE

Elevation: 9,627 ft.

Outlet: 39° 59' 49.09" N	**107° 13'**	**48.30" W**
Scotts Bay: 39° 59' 18.85" N	**107° 14'**	**13.69" W**

» 320 acres; 180 feet deep; brook and cutthroat trout.

» The Big Fish Fire of 2002 burned a very significant amount of timber around much of the lake. Regardless of the burn, fishing was good again by fall. Only a few campsites in the Trappers Lake Campground were damaged.

» Take FR 205 10 miles to outlet parking area and trailhead. To reach the campground and Scotts Bay Trailhead, go 9 miles on FR 205 to FR 209, then west 1.5 miles.

» Fishing is permitted with flies and lures only. All cutthroat over

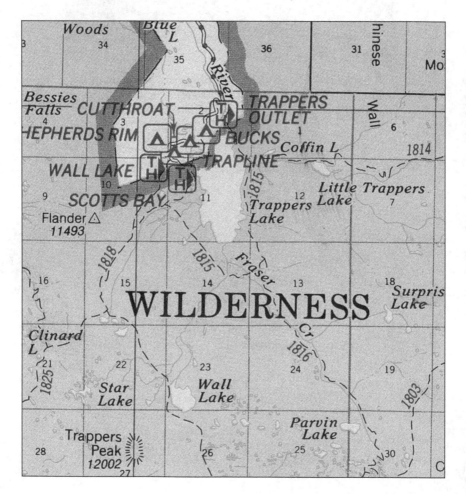

Trappers and Wall Lakes

10 inches must be released. Anglers are requested by Colorado Parks and Wildlife to keep all brook trout caught. Fishing is prohibited within 100 feet of all inlets and the outlet. The closures are marked.

COFFIN LAKE

Elevation: 9,710 ft. **39° 59′ 31.12″ N** **107° 13′ 16.96″ W**

» 30 acres; cutthroat trout.
» Reported that CPW sometimes stocks brood trout here. Some up to 5 pounds and they are difficult to catch.
» The north shoreline is steep and the south is heavily wooded, making casting a fly rod a challenge. That was before the Big Fish Fire of 2002, which burned all around the lake.
» Take FR 205 10 miles to outlet parking area and trailhead. Trail 1815 follows the east shoreline of Trappers Lake. At the CPW cabins, take Trail 1814 (39° 59′ 29.64 N, 107° 13′ 28.05″ W) east 0.5 mile to Coffin.

LITTLE TRAPPERS LAKE

Elevation: 9,926 ft. **39° 59′ 49.09″ N** **107° 12′ 35.83″ W**

» 20 acres; 22 feet deep; cutthroat trout.
» The north shoreline is open and easy to cast from, but a shallow shelf makes it difficult to reach deeper water. Good for fishing from a float tube, as the south shore is deeper and lined with dense forest.
» Take FR 205 10 miles to outlet parking area and trailhead. Trail 1815 follows the east shoreline of Trappers Lake. At the CPW cabins, take Trail 1814 east to Little Trappers.

SURPRISE LAKE

Elevation: 11,128 ft.	39° 57' 56.84" N	107° 11' 31.64" W

» 9 acres; 37 feet deep; cutthroat stocked in 2001.

» Take Trail 1814 1 mile past Little Trappers Lake, (to 39° 59' 30.47" N, 107° 11' 11.49" W) then go cross-country 2 miles south to Surprise Lake. No trail. Surprise Lake was not affected by the 2002 fires.

WALL LAKE

Elevation: 10,986 ft.	39° 57' 08.22" N	107° 14' 31.34" W

» 45 acres; 21 feet deep; cutthroat trout stocked in 2001.

» A shallow shelf extends out into the lake just far enough to make it difficult to cast to the deeper water. This is a good lake to fish from a float tube. It's best early and late in the day.

» FR 209 to Wall Lake Trailhead, 0.5 mile from Trappers Lake Campground. Travel 5 miles on Trail 1818 to the lake.

Forest Road 8 : Ripple Creek Pass

CR 8 changes its designation at the west boundary of the White River National Forest, 9 miles east of Buford. At FR 205, the road climbs to Ripple Creek Pass. A quarter mile west of the pass, a parking area gives access to wilderness trails to the south, and the roadless area to the north. Pagoda Peak, a good landmark, is visible 3 miles to the north.

PAGODA LAKE

Elevation: 10,313 ft.	40° 07' 51.78" N	107° 20' 52.53" W

» 15 acres; 15 feet deep; brook trout stocked in 1996.

» A quarter mile on the west side of Ripple Creek Pass is the Lost

Lake Pagoda Trailhead. Take Trail 1804 4 miles to the lake. After June 15th, the trail is open for use by ATVs and motorcycles, but other motorized transportation is prohibited. Well-known by local anglers so gets a lot of pressure on weekends.

3

ROUTT COUNTY

Forest Road 16

At the summit of Ripple Creek Pass, which is also the county line, the roadbecomes FR 16.

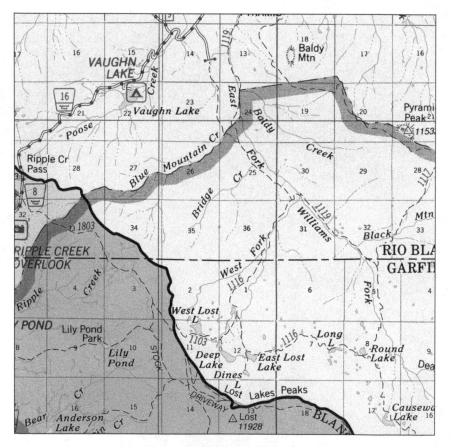

Ripple Creek Pass, Lost Lakes, Long, Round, and Causeway Lakes

Elevation: 9,390 ft.   **40° 07′ 57.22″ N**   **107° 15′ 32.61″ W**

- » 36 acres; 24 feet deep; rainbow trout.
- » The lake is 3 miles east of Ripple Creek Pass on the south side of the road. There is a small USFS campground. The fishing is maintained by stocking.

Vaughn Lake is a put-and-take fishery beside Forest Road 16 east of Ripple Creek Pass.

Williams Fork

Three miles east of Vaughn Lake on FR 16, Transfer Trail Road heads south 1 mile. From here, Trail 1119 parallels the East Fork of the Williams Fork. Along the trail, Baldy, Blue Mountain, Bridge, West Fork, and Black Mountain Creeks join the Williams Fork. All are small but have fish, primarily cutthroat trout.

Small creeks like this one often hide nice surprises for anglers.

WEST LOST LAKE

Elevation: 10,296 ft.　　　**40° 04' 20.73" N**　　　**107° 14' 10.25" W**

» 18 acres; 32 feet deep; brook trout.

» Fish are better than average size, but can be challenging to catch.

» From the end of the Transfer Trail Road, take Trail 1119 south 3 miles to Trail 1116, then southwest 4 miles to Trail 1103, and west 0.5 mile to West Lost Lake. An alternate route is Trail 1803 from the Lost Lake Pagoda Trailhead. Head south 5 miles, then east 0.5 mile to the lake.

» The lake is also accessible from Stillwater Reservoir. Take Trail 1119 8 miles to Trail 1116, then 3 miles to Trail 1103, and 1.25 miles to West Lost Lake.

DEEP LAKE

Elevation: 10,250 ft.   40° 04′ 06.82″ N   107° 13′ 43.89″ W

» 23 acres; 54 feet deep; brook trout.

» From the end of the Transfer Trail Road, take Trail 1119 south 3 miles to Trail 1116, then southwest 4 miles to Trail 1103, and south 0.1 mile to Deep Lake.

» From Lost Lake Pagoda Trailhead, head south 5 miles on Trail 1803, then east on Trail 1103 1 mile to the lake.

» From Stillwater Reservoir, take Trail 1119 8 miles to Trail 1116, 1 mile to the East Lost Lake, then 1 mile south to the lake; or follow the inlet creek upstream one-quarter mile to Deep Lake. It's shorter than following the trails, but goes through thick down timber.

DINES LAKE

Elevation: 10,350 ft.   40° 03′ 48.81″ N   107° 13′ 16.57″ W

» 6 acres; 4 feet deep; cutthroat trout.

» From the end of the Transfer Trail Road, take Trail 1119 south 3 miles to Trail 1116, then 0.25 mile south at the south end of East Lost Lake to Dines. Also accessible from Stillwater Reservoir. Trail 1119 8 miles to Trail 1116, 1 mile to East Lost Lake, then south one-quarter mile to Dines.

EAST LOST LAKE

Elevation: 10,300 ft.   40° 04′ 05.20″ N   107° 13′ 14.00″ W

» 18 acres; 32 feet deep; cutthroat trout stocked in 2001.

» From the end of the Transfer Trail Road, take Trail 1119 south 3 miles to Trail 1116, then 3 miles south to East Lost Lake.

Lakes like this one are found throughout the wilderness.

» From Stillwater Reservoir, take Trail 1119 8 miles to Trail 1116, and follow 1 mile to the lake.

LONG LAKE

Elevation: 10,464 ft.	**40° 04' 07.78" N**	**107° 11' 39.76" W**

» 11 acres; 8 feet deep; cutthroat trout stocked in 2001.
» It's difficult to fish from the shoreline because of dense timber to the water's edge, except on the north end. A good lake for using a float tube.
» From the end of the Transfer Trail Road, take Trail 1119 south 3 miles to Trail 1116, then 6 miles south to Long Lake.
» From Stillwater Reservoir, take Trail 1119 8 miles to the lake.

Long Lake is home to better than average cutts.

ROUND LAKE

Elevation: 10,360 ft.   **40° 04′ 03.30″ N**   **107° 10′ 57.39″ W**

» 8 acres; 17 feet deep; cutthroat trout stocked in 2001.
» From the end of the Transfer Trail Road, take Trail 1119 south
   3 miles to Trail 1116, then go 7 miles south to Round Lake.
   A shorter route to Round is Trail 1119, a distance of 8 miles.
» From Stillwater Reservoir, take Trail 1119 7 miles to the lake.

CAUSEWAY LAKE

Elevation: 10,430 ft.   **40° 03′ 12.77″ N**   **107° 10′ 27.84″ W**

» 24 acres; 5 feet deep; cutthroat trout.
» The lake looks like a very large beaver pond.

An angler prepares to tempt a Causeway Lake cutthroat.

» From the end of the Transfer Trail Road, take Trail 1119 south 9 miles to Causeway.

» From Stillwater Reservoir, take Trail 1119 5 miles to the lake.

Forest Road 959

FR 945 heads south from FR 16. It is located 22 miles east of Ripple Creek Pass and 13 miles west of Yampa. The road ends at Sheriff Reservoir. Several lakes and streams are accessed from the road.

TROUT CREEK

» The stream heads below Orno Peak 6 miles southeast of Sheriff Reservoir. It's a small stream with a high gradient. Lots of pocket water to fish for rainbow trout, both north and south of FR 16.

Anglers will find lots of pocket water in Trout Creek.

RAINBOW LAKE

Elevation: 9,700 ft. **40° 09' 09.51" N** **107° 08' 01.03" W**

» 1 acre; 22 feet deep; cutthroat and rainbow trout.

» The lake is located 3 miles south on FR 945 and one-quarter mile east of the road across Trout Creek.

SHERIFF RESERVOIR

Elevation: 9,723 ft. **40° 08' 55.72" N** **107° 08' 16.19" W**

» 40 acres; 43 feet deep; brook trout reported in the past, and rainbow trout stocked in 2001.

» Travel 4 miles south on FR 945 to the end of the road. There is a campground on the west side of Sheriff Reservoir.

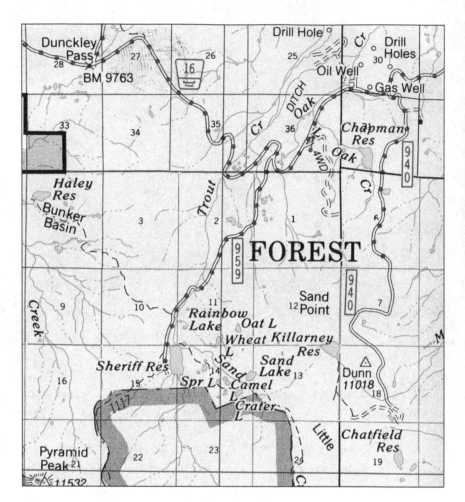

Sheriff Reservoir

SPRING LAKE

Elevation: 10,070 ft.   **40° 08′ 33.92″ N**   **107° 07′ 29.20″ W**

» 2 acres; 7 feet deep; brook, cutthroat, and rainbow trout.

» From the dam at Sheriff Reservoir, hike southeast on the trail
0.5 mile to Spring Lake.

A rough 4-wheel-drive road leads to Sheriff Reservoir.

CAMEL LAKE

Elevation: 10,100 ft.   **40° 08' 32.80" N**   **107° 07' 21.80" W**

» 2 acres; 5 feet deep; brook and cutthroat trout.
» The lake is 1 mile southeast on the trail from Sheriff Reservoir dam.

CRATER LAKE

Elevation: 10,150 ft.   **40° 08' 26.22" N**   **107° 07' 09.11" W**

» 4 acres; 10 feet deep; no report of fish.
» The lake is 0.1 mile from Camel Lake.

SAND LAKE

Elevation: 10,192 ft.   **40° 08' 32.41" N**   **107° 07' 05.73" W**

» 2 acres; 12 feet deep; brook trout.
» The lake is 1 mile southeast of Sheriff Reservoir dam.

WHEAT LAKE

Elevation: 9,930 ft.   **40° 08′ 55.10″ N**   **107° 07′ 34.66″ W**

» 3 acres; 4 feet deep; cutthroat and rainbow trout.
» The lake is 0.5 mile east of Sheriff Reservoir dam and upstream from Rainbow Lake.

OAT LAKE

Elevation: 10,150 ft.   **40° 09′ 07.24″ N**   **107° 07′ 16.34″ W**

» 6 acres; 4 feet deep; cutthroat and rainbow trout.
» From Wheat Lake, go cross-country 0.5 mile northeast.

Forest Road 940

FR 940 heads south from FR 16, and is located 25 miles east of Ripple Creek Pass and 10 miles west of Yampa.

CHAPMAN RESERVOIR

Elevation: 9,280 ft.   **40° 11′ 12.07″ N**   **107° 05′ 19.68″ W**

» 25 acres; 26 feet deep; rainbow trout stocked in 2000.
» Boats allowed, but only electric trolling motors permitted.
» Located 2 miles south on FR 940.

CHATFIELD RESERVOIR

Elevation: 10,515 ft.   **40° 07′ 47.53″ N**   **107° 04′ 49.03″ W**

» 13 acres; 20 feet deep; cutthroat trout.
» Travel 6 miles south on FR 940 to 40° 08′ 05.63″ N, 107° 04′ 48.31″ W, then 0.5 mile south cross-country to the reservoir.

KILLARNEY RESERVOIR

Elevation: 10,943 ft.   **40° 08' 47.32" N**   **107° 05' 43.27" W**

» No information.

» Travel 7 miles south to end of FR 940, then follow the trail 1 mile north to the reservoir.

County Road 17

This road heads west on the north side of Yampa and links with CR 132, which becomes FR 16 inside Routt National Forest.

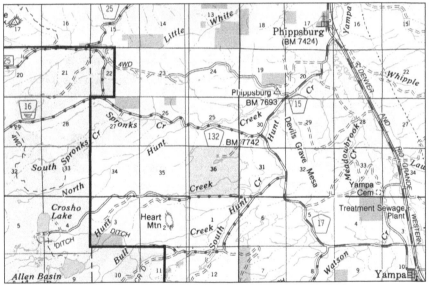

Crosho Lake and Allen Basin Reservoir

CROSHO LAKE

Elevation: 8,910 ft.   **40° 10' 12.75" N**   **107° 03' 13.93" W**

» 56 acres; 75 feet deep; cutthroat trout and grayling, which were stocked in 1992.

Crosho Lake is one of the few places in Colorado where anglers take grayling.

» Located 4 miles east of CR 17 on Road 15.
» Crosho Reservoir produced a catch-and-release record in 1996, a grayling of 15.5 inches. Again in 1998 Crosho produced another 15 incher, along with a 16 incher. The lake offers a good chance to take a Master Angler qualifying grayling (15 inches or longer).

ALLEN BASIN RESERVOIR

Elevation: 8,700 ft.   **40° 09′ 40.98″ N**   **107° 02′ 30.21″ W**

» 70 acres; brook trout stocked in 1995, and rainbow trout stocked in 1994.
» This is a fluctuating irrigation reservoir, but offers good fishing.
» Travel 4 miles east of CR 17 on Road 15, then hike south 1 mile on the trail.

County Road 7 (Forest Road 900): Bear (Yampa) River

On the southwest end of Yampa, County Road 7 follows the Bear River to Stillwater Reservoir. At the forest boundary, the road becomes Forest Road 900. From the boundary to its headwaters, the stream runs through public land. It has brook, brown, and rainbow trout, and whitefish.

At Yampa, the Bear River becomes the Yampa River. There is no public access until it flows into Stagecoach Reservoir.

Below Stagecoach Dam, the Yampa is a neat tailwater stream. It offers public access on a half mile of water, plus another mile at Service Creek State Wildlife Area. Special regulations include angling with flies and lures only between Stagecoach Dam and the inlet to Catamount Lake, and all fish caught must be released unharmed.

Several miles of tailwater angling are available on the Bear River.

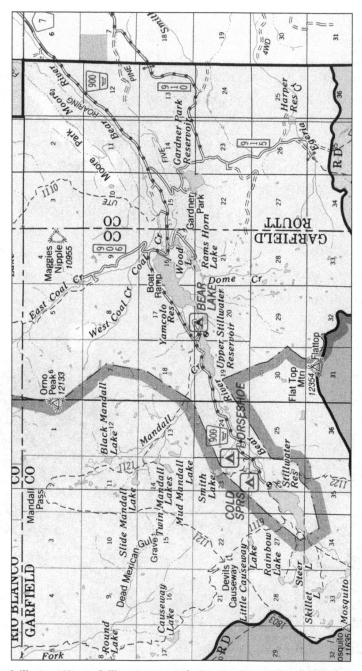

Stillwater, Upper Stillwater, Yamcola Reservoirs, and Mandall Lakes

GARDNER PARK RESERVOIR

Elevation: 9,630 ft.   **40° 03′ 00.27″ N**   **107° 01′ 02.58″ W**

» 65 acres; rainbow trout stocked in 2001; sometimes winterkills.
» Located 11 miles west of Yampa on CR 7 and FR 900 to FR 915,
south 4 miles to reservoir.

HARPER RESERVOIR

Elevation: 9,820 ft.   **40° 01′ 20.35″ N**   **107° 00′ 00.75″ W**

» Brook trout.
» Located 11 miles west of Yampa on CR 7 and FR 900 to FR 915,
south 4 miles past Gardner Park Reservoir, then 0.5 mile east to
Harper Reservoir.

SUNNYSIDE LAKES

Elevation: 10,300 ft.   **39° 59′ 47.34″ N**   **107° 01′ 12.09″ W**

» 10 acres total; 4 to 5 feet deep; brook trout.
» Located 11 miles west of Yampa on CR 7 and FR 900 to FR 915,
south 4 miles past Gardner Park Reservoir, then a quarter mile
past the turnoff to Harper Reservoir, south to Trail 1861 to lakes.

HEART LAKE

Elevation: 9,947 ft.   **40° 03′ 35.44″ N**   **107° 02′ 36.18″ W**

» 24 acres; 18 feet deep; rainbow and cutthroat trout both stocked
in 2001.
» Reported to have good feed conditions to grow large fish.
» Located 11 miles west of Yampa on CR 7 and FR 900 to spur

leading to 1110. Go 7 miles to the lake. Other lakes along the trail are Blue Lake (no fish), Bull Park (no report), Bull Park Reservoir (no report), and McChivvis Reservoir (no report).

WOOD LAKE

Elevation: 9,680 ft.   **40° 02' 53.26" N**   **107° 02' 36.69" W**

» 5 acres; 15 feet deep; brook trout.
» Travel 14 miles west of Yampa on CR 7 and FR 900, then south on access road before reaching Yamcola Reservoir.

RAMS HORN LAKE

Elevation: 9,820 ft.   **40° 02' 48.04" N**   **107° 02' 41.96" W**

» 15 acres; 14 feet deep; brook and rainbow trout.
» Travel 14 miles west of Yampa on CR 7 and FR 900, then south on access road before reaching Yamcola Reservoir.

YAMCOLA RESERVOIR

Elevation: 9,600 ft.   **40° 03' 13.65" N**   **107° 02' 42.76" W**

» 168 acres; brook, brown, rainbow, and mackinaw trout, and whitefish. Rainbows stocked in 2000.
» Located 14 miles west of Yampa on CR 7 and FR 900.
» There are 7 Mandall Lakes, but only the following have fish. All are inside the Flat Tops Wilderness, so access is by foot or horseback only.

Brushy banks make casting a challenge, but provide cover for the trout.

MUD MANDALL LAKE

Elevation: 10,550 ft.   **40° 02′ 59.90″ N**   **107° 06′ 45.07″ W**

- » 2 acres; 3 feet deep; brook, cutthroat, and rainbow trout.
- » Travel 14 miles west of Yampa on CR 7 and FR 900, then 2 miles northwest on Trail 1121.

TWIN MANDALL LAKES

Elevation: 10,550 ft.   **40° 03′ 24.28″ N**   **107° 06′ 55.66″ W**

- » Lower: 5 acres; 5 feet deep; brook and rainbow trout reported in the past. Cutthroat trout stocked in 1994.
- » Upper: 8 acres; 15 feet deep; brook and rainbow trout.
- » Travel 14 miles west of Yampa on CR 7 and FR 900, then 2.5 miles northwest on Trail 1121.

SLIDE MANDALL LAKE

Elevation: 10,625 ft.   40° 03' 41.31" N   107° 07' 09.00" W

» Cutthroat trout stocked in 1994.

» Travel 14 miles west of Yampa on CR 7 and FR 900, then 2.5 miles northwest on Trail 1121.

BLACK MANDALL LAKE

Elevation: 10,770 ft.   40° 04' 10.64" N 107°   06' 55.30" W

» 9 acres; 11 feet deep; rainbow trout stocked in 1994, and cutthroat trout stocked in 2001.

» Travel 14 miles west of Yampa on CR 7 and FR 900, then 3 miles northwest on Trail 1121.

UPPER STILLWATER (YAMPA) RESERVOIR

Elevation: 9,750 ft.   40° 02' 46.25" N   107° 04' 25.78" W

» 47 acres; brook, cutthroat, and rainbow trout, and whitefish.

» Handicapped access on part of the shoreline.

» Located 15 miles west of Yampa on CR 7 and FR 900.

SMITH LAKE

Elevation: 10,500 ft.   40° 02' 20.28" N   107° 07' 09.06" W

» 11 acres; 12 feet deep; brook trout, and cutthroat trout stocked in 1996.

» 17 miles west of Yampa on CR 7 and FR 900, park at Cold Springs Campground. Hike 0.5 mile north on access trail.

Smith Lake is a short, easy hike from the trailhead.
Take plenty of insect repellent.

STILLWATER RESERVOIR

Elevation: 10,255 ft.   **40° 01′ 37.42″ N**   **107° 07′ 26.27″ W**

» Stillwater Reservoir is 17 miles west of Yampa on CR 7 and FR 900. 165 acres when full; 52 feet deep; brook and cutthroat reported in the past; rainbow trout stocked in 2000.

» Boat ramp. Boats are allowed, but only electric trolling motors are permitted for power. Campgrounds are nearby.

SUNNYSIDE LAKES

Elevation: 10,390 ft.   **39° 59′ 47.34″ N**   **107° 01′ 12.09″ W**

» 10 acres; 4 to 5 feet deep; brook trout.

» Travel 11 miles west of Yampa on CR 7 and FR 900 to FR 915, south 4 miles past Gardner Park Reservoir, then a quarter mile beyond the turnoff to Harper Reservoir, and south to end of the road, where it connects to Trail 1861 leading to the lakes.

MOSQUITO LAKE

Elevation: 10,620 ft.   **40° 00′ 20.66″ N**   **107° 09′ 01.03″ W**

» 10 acres; 6 feet deep; brook trout; cutthroat trout stocked in 2003.
» 17 miles west of Yampa on CR 7 and FR 900, park at Stillwater Reservoir. Hike 2 miles southwest on Trail 1814.

SKILLET LAKE

Elevation: 10,700 ft.   **40° 00′ 45.38″ N**   **107° 09′ 27.02″ W**

» 8 acres; 6 feet deep; brook trout.
» 17 miles west of Yampa on CR 7 and FR 900, park at Stillwater Reservoir. Hike 1.5 miles southwest on Trail 1814, then 0.5 mile west on the access trail.

RAINBOW LAKE

Elevation: 10,764 ft.   **40° 01′ 26.35″ N**   **107° 09′ 12.69″ W**

» 1 acre; 22 feet deep; cutthroat and rainbow trout.
» 17 miles west of Yampa on CR 7 and FR 900, park at Stillwater Reservoir. Hike 1 mile southwest on Trail 1814, then 1 mile west on access trail.
» The following lakes can also be accessed from Stump Park by taking FR 610 off CR 39 out of Burns or Derby Junction from Eagle CR 309. FR 610 is a very rough road and small 4-wheel-drive vehicles are best here. From the trailhead of Trail 1860, the distance to all lakes is 5 to 6 miles.

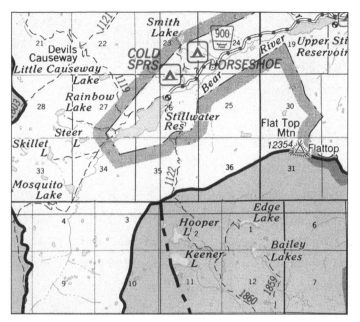

Hooper, Keener, Edge, and Bailey Lakes

HOOPER LAKE

Elevation: 10,864 ft.   **39° 59' 38.28" N**   **107° 07' 01.77" W**

» 22 acres; 10 feet deep; brook trout stocked in 1995; cutthroat trout stocked in 1993.

» 17 miles west of Yampa on CR 7 and FR 900, park at Stillwater Reservoir. Cross the dam, then go south 3 miles on Trail 1122 and 1860 (the trail number changes at the Routt/White River National Forest boundary) to lake.

KEENER LAKE

Elevation: 10,780 ft.   **39° 59' 17.18" N**   **107° 06' 59.63" W**

» 12 acres; 30 feet deep; cutthroat trout stocked in 1993; rainbow trout stocked in 1994.

» 17 miles west of Yampa on CR 7 and FR 900, park at Stillwater Reservoir. Cross the dam, then go south 3 miles on Trail 1122 and 1860 (the trail number changes at the Flat Tops Wilderness Area boundary) to Hooper Lake, then 0.5 mile south to Keener.

EDGE LAKE

Elevation: 10,910 ft.	39° 59' 51.93" N	107° 06' 04.35" W

» 17 acres; brook trout; cutthroat trout stocked in 1994.
» 17 miles west of Yampa on CR 7 and FR 900, park at Stillwater Reservoir. Cross the dam, then south 3 miles on Trail 1122 and 1860 (trail number changes at the Routt/White River boundary) to Trail 1859, then 1 mile northeast.

BAILEY LAKES

Elevation: 10,798 ft.	39° 59' 32.82" N	107° 05' 49.01" W

» Approximately 5 acres; brook trout.
» 17 miles west of Yampa on CR 7 and FR 900, park at Stillwater Reservoir. Cross the dam, then go south 3 miles on Trail 1122 and 1860 (the trail number changes at the Routt/White River county boundary) to Trail 1859, then 1 mile northeast to Edge Lake, and south 0.5 mile to Bailey Lakes.

4

EAGLE COUNTY

Middle Fork Derby Creek: Eagle County Road 39

The Middle Fork is within the wilderness boundary. Reports are that it's excellent for brook trout.

The following lakes are accessed from Stump Park taking FR 610 off CR 39 out of Burns or Derby Junction from Eagle CR 301. FR 610 is a very rough road and small 4-wheel-drive vehicles are best here.

ROAD LAKE

Elevation: 10,204 ft.   **39° 57′ 56.52″ N**   **107° 04′ 59.26″ W**

» From Stump Park trailhead, take Trail 1860 2 miles to the lake.

SOLITARY LAKE

Elevation: 10,638 ft.   **39° 57′ 49.07″ N**   **107° 06′ 14.36″ W**

» 12 acres; 16 feet deep; brook and rainbow trout.
» From Stump Park trailhead, take Trail 1846 3 miles to the lake.

MUSKRAT LAKE

Elevation: 10,230 ft.   **39° 57′ 01.66″ N**   **107° 07′ 17.48″ W**

» 5 acres; 4 feet deep; rainbow trout.
» From Stump Park trailhead, take Trail 1846 2 miles, then Trail 1842 2 miles to the lake.

South Fork Derby Creek:
Eagle County Road 39

The South Fork is worth fishing for brook trout. Downstream from Crescent Lake, the stream also has cutthroat trout.

The following lakes are accessed from CR 39 out of Burns or Derby Junction. Take FR 613, a rough four-wheel drive road, through Deer Park. The road crosses the South Fork of Derby Creek and continues west to Crescent and Mackinaw Lakes. After passing Emerald Lake, a short wheelbase vehicle is best because of the road's steep dips and tight turns. This section of the road gets very slick after any rain.

EMERALD LAKE

Elevation: 9,548 ft.	39° 54′ 11.41″ N	107° 06′ 9.59″ W

- » 10 acres; 9 feet deep; brook trout.
- » Take FR 610 8 miles past CR 39.

STILL WATERS

Elevation: 9,790 ft.	39° 54′ 00.60″ N	107° 05′ 49.26″ W

- » 9 acres; 4 feet deep; brook trout.
- » Take FR 610 9 miles past CR 39.

CRESCENT LAKE

Elevation: 10,758 ft.	39° 54′ 26.84″ N	107° 09′ 12.54″ W

- » 38 acres; 39 feet deep; brook, cutthroat, mackinaw, and rainbow trout.
- » Take FR 610 12 miles past CR 39.

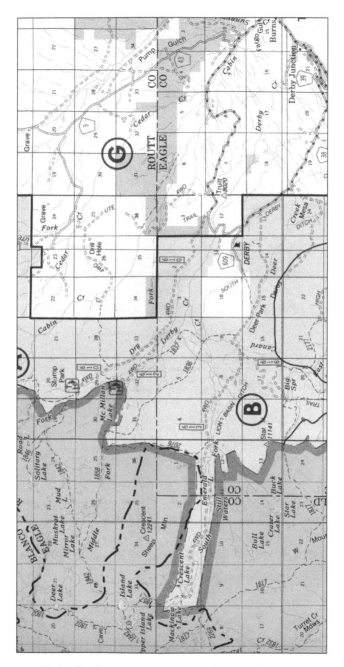

Derby Creek, Crescent Lakes, Mackinaw Lakes, Island Lakes, and Deer Lake

MACKINAW LAKE

Elevation: 10,766 ft.   **39° 54' 37.16" N**   **107° 09' 32.09" W**

» 8 acres; 14 feet deep; brook, cutthroat, mackinaw, and rainbow trout.
» Take FR 610 13 miles past CR 39.

Island Lakes

The Island Lakes can be accessed from FR 610 at Mackinaw Lake, 2 miles along Trail 1857. The 3 lakes are within a quarter mile of each other.

LOWER ISLAND LAKE

Elevation: 10,866 ft.   **39° 59' 56.57" N**   **107° 09' 52.55" W**

» 28 acres; 21 feet deep; cutthroat trout stocked in 2001.

MIDDLE ISLAND LAKE

Elevation: 11,180 ft.   **39° 55' 51.87" N**   **107° 10' 14.54" W**

» 15 acres; 13 feet deep; cutthroat stocked in 1992; rainbow trout reported in the past.

UPPER ISLAND LAKE

Elevation: 11,202 ft.   **39° 55' 41.82" N**   **107° 10' 9.58" W**

» 27 acres; 45 feet deep; cutthroat trout stocked in 2001; rainbow trout reported in the past.

DEER LAKE

Elevation: 11,130 ft.   **39° 59' 56.57" N**   **107° 09' 52.55" W**

» 3 acres; 53 feet deep; cutthroat trout stocked in 2001.
» From FR 610 at Mackinaw Lake, go 2 miles on Trail 1857 to Middle Island Lake, then 3 miles north on Trail 1802.

Sweetwater Creek

Sweetwater Creek heads in the wilderness area near Shingle Peak. The stream runs through private land downstream from Sweetwater Lake, and is generally not open to public fishing. Rim and Shepherd Lakes, south of Shingle Peak, are the source of Sweetwater Creek. They are more easily accessed from FR 600, which leaves CR 301 at Deep Creek, 2 miles north of Dotsero on Interstate 70.

SWEETWATER LAKE

Elevation: 7,709 ft.   **39° 47' 59.02" N**   **107° 09' 34.06" W**

» 80 acres; brook trout; cutthroat and rainbow trout stocked in 2001.
» 10 miles from CR 309 on CR 12.
» Boats allowed, motors prohibited.
» Camping at Sweetwater Campground south of the lake.
» A lodge has rooms and a restaurant.

Forest Road 600: Deep Creek

Deep Creek heads in Deep Lake and joins the Colorado River 2 miles north of Dotsero. The creek runs along FR 600 for 2 miles before the road swings away. It's a small, fast creek with lots of pocket water. The best fishing is reported to be in Deep Creek Canyon, a half-mile-deep gorge

with little access. The stream has brook and cutthroat trout.
The following lakes are accessed from FR 600.

DEEP LAKE

Elevation: 10,462 ft.   **39° 46′ 21.54″ N**   **107° 18′ 05.98″ W**

» 37 acres; 65 feet deep; brook trout; cutthroat and rainbow trout stocked in 2001.
» Located 30 miles from CR 301 on FR 600. Includes campground and water.
» Park at the trailhead to Trail 1816, at Indian Camp Pass. From the trailhead, it's 5 miles to Indian Lake, 7 miles to Shepherd Lake, and 8 miles to Rim Lake.

INDIAN LAKE

Elevation: 10,558 ft.   **39° 51′ 34.74″ N**   **107° 15′ 52.52″ W**

» 15 acres; 8 feet deep; cutthroat trout stocked in 2001.

SHEPHERD LAKE

Elevation: 10,762 ft.   **39° 57′ 38.52″ N**   **107° 14′ 44.45″ W**

» 30 acres; 18 feet deep; brook trout stocked in 1995; cutthroat trout stocked in 2001; mackinaw trout reported in the past.

RIM LAKE

Elevation: 10,804 ft.   **39° 52′ 46.75″ N**   **107° 14′ 58.77″ W**

» 14 acres; 37 feet deep; cutthroat trout stocked in 2001; mackinaw trout stocked in 1994.

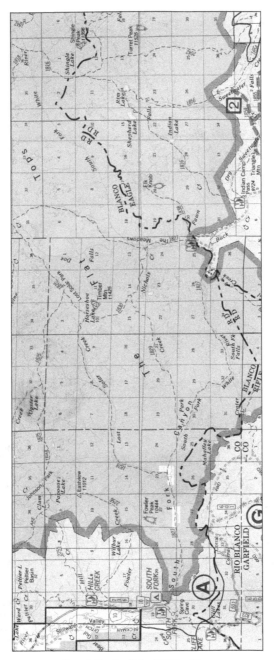

South Fork of the White River

Elevation: 11,214 ft.   **39° 52′ 46.75″ N**   **107° 14′ 58.77″ W**

» Cutthroat trout stocked in 1996.

South Fork of the White River

The parking area and trailhead for the headwaters of the South Fork is 3 miles past Indian Camp Pass Trailhead.

Trail 1827 heads north from the parking lot upstream, following the river for 3 miles. An undesignated path parallels the stream for another 7 miles to its origin. The path is not maintained, but it gets enough traffic to keep it visible and easy to follow.

Access to the river along the first mile, near The Meadows, is a challenge. From the trail, the willows growing along the White don't look bad—they're almost impenetrable, though.

The logjam created a good fishing-holding pool.

All angling methods are legal, but fly fishing this section is usually the most productive method. One interesting thing about the river is that even if there is no hatch occurring, brook trout will usually take a dry fly. Anglers will find beaver ponds in several places along the sides of the river. These sometimes produce cutthroats.

To fish the middle section of the South Fork, continue another 1.5 miles to a second trailhead. The river gets continually larger as it is fed by numerous side streams. Brook trout are common from The Meadows downstream another 4 miles, although the river also has cutthroat and rainbows. For a backpack trip, begin at The Meadows or the next trailhead, and fish the river until you come out at the South Fork Campground, 13 miles downstream. The fish tend to get larger toward the campground.

Other small creeks in the area include Buck, Dry Buck, Fawn, Nichols, and Doe.

The following lakes are accessed from FR 600, 29 miles from CR 301 to FR 645. Four-wheel drive is recommended for all roads in this area.

HEART LAKE

Elevation: 10,708 ft. **39° 46' 02.57" N** **107° 18' 59.97" W**

» 480 acres; 20 feet deep; brook trout stocked in 1994; mackinaw trout stocked in 1993.
» Go west 2 miles on FR 645. The lake is north of the road.

KLINES FOLLY

Elevation: 10,660 ft. **39° 45' 33.76" N** **107° 18' 37.55" W**

» 4 acres; 17 feet deep; cutthroat and rainbow trout; often winterkills.
» Go west 2 miles on FR 645. The lake is south of the road.

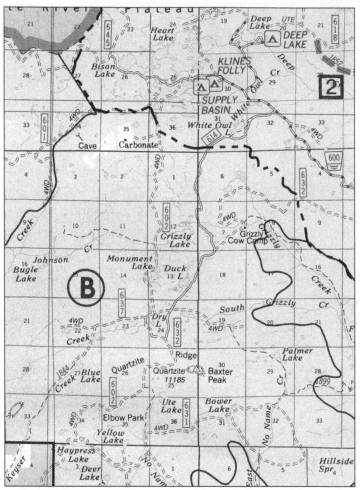

Deep Lake and Grizzly Lake

SUPPLY BASIN

Elevation: 10,750 ft.   **39° 45′ 33.28″ N**   **107° 19′ 11.66″ W**

» 5 acres; 28 feet deep; rainbow trout.
» Go west 2 miles on FR 645, then south 0.5 mile on the access road. The lake is south of FR 645.

BISON LAKE

Elevation: 10,746 ft.   **39° 46′ 44.98″ N**   **107° 20′ 41.51″ W**

- » 20 acres; rainbow trout.
- » Go west 2.5 miles on FR 645.

The following lakes are accessed by very rough, 4-wheel-drive roads.

GRIZZLY LAKE

Elevation: 10,670 ft.   **39° 42′ 59.82″ N**   **107° 19′ 08.98″ W**

- » 15 acres; 12 feet deep; brook trout; often winterkills.
- » Take FR 614 southwest 4 miles to the lake.

DUCK LAKE

Elevation: 10,690 ft.   **39° 41′ 56.95″ N**   **107° 19′ 15.55″ W**

- » 12 acres; 25 feet deep; brook trout.
- » Take FR 614 southwest 5 miles to the lake.

MONUMENT LAKE

Elevation: 10,750 ft.   **39° 42′ 00.06″ N**   **107° 20′ 10.28″ W**

- » 13 acres; brook trout; often winterkills.
- » Take FR 614 south 7 miles, then head northwest 1 mile on FR 632, and north 1 mile on FR 602.

HAYPRESS LAKE

Elevation: 10,390 ft.   **39° 39′ 06.20″ N**   **107° 21′ 35.87″ W**

- » 6 acres; cutthroat trout.

» Take FR 614 south 7 miles, then go 5 miles on FR 602 to the lake.

YELLOW LAKE

Elevation: 10,360 ft.   **39° 39′ 01.23″ N**   **107° 20′ 42.30″ W**

» 8 acres; 26 feet deep; brook trout.
» From FR 614, go 6 miles on FR 602 past Haypress Lake to the access road, then north 0.5 mile to Yellow Lake.

BLUE LAKE

Elevation: 10,420 ft.   **39° 40′ 34.00″ N**   **107° 21′ 52.38″ W**

» 8 acres; 12 feet deep; brook trout.
» From FR 614, go west on FR 637 3 miles to Blue Lake.
» Several small streams are in this area—Grizzly, No Name, Canyon Creeks—and their branches generally run south. Grizzly is the largest. This river and its forks are difficult to reach because of rugged country, but are reported to have brook and rainbow trout.
» West of Bison Lake, FR 645 connects with FR 640 and gives access to a trail leading to Jet, Shadow, Blair, Crater, and Mahaffey Lakes. FR 640 is very rough and rocky. It is not recommended, especially for large four-wheel drive vehicles. A better route to these lakes is from the Buford–New Castle Road, CR 59.

Wilderness Lodges and Outfitters

Adams Lodge Outfitters
6389 County Road 4, PO Box 1377
Meeker, CO 81641
(970) 878-4312
www.adamslodgeoutfitters.com

Pollard's Ute Lodge
393 County Road 75
Meeker, CO 81641
(970) 878-4669
www.utelodge.com

Ripple Creek Lodge
39020 County Road 8
Meeker, CO 81641
(970) 878-4725
www.ripplecreeklodge.com

**Trappers Lake Lodge &
Resort**
7700 Trappers Lake Road
Meeker, CO 81641
(970) 878-3336 or (970) 878-5288
www.trapperslake.com

**Budge's Flattops
Wilderness Lodge**
 (901) 466-2265
budges@budgeslodge.com
www.budgeslodge.com

Information Resources

Colorado Fishing Network
Fishing Information,
Fly Shops, Guides
www.coloradofishing.net

Colorado Parks and Wildlife
6060 Broadway
Denver, CO
(303) 291-7227
www.wildlife.state.co.us

0088 Wildlife Way
Glenwood Springs, CO 81601
(970) 947-2920

US Forest Service
National Forest Maps
740 Simms St.
Golden, CO 80401
(303) 275-5350
www.fs.fed.us/recreation/map/

Bureau of Land Management
Colorado Surface Ownership Maps
2850 Youngfield St.
Lakewood, CO 80215
(303) 239-3600
www.blm.gov/co/st/en.html

US Geological Survey Real Time
Colorado Stream Flows
www.waterdata.usgs.gov/co/nwis/

Colorado Division of
Water Resources
www.dwr.state.co.us/SurfaceWater/

FEDERAL AGENCIES
US Forest Service
Rocky Mountain Regional Office
740 Simms St.
Golden, CO 80401
(303) 275-5350

White River National Forest
Supervisor
Old Federal Building
PO Box 848
Glenwood Springs, CO 81601
(970) 945-2521

Blanco Ranger District
(White River NF)
317 E. Market
PO Box 358
Meeker, CO 81641
(970) 878-4039

Eagle Ranger District
(White River NF)
125 W. 5th St.
PO Box 720
Eagle, CO 81631
(970) 328-6388

Rifle Ranger District
(White River NF)
0094 County Road 244
Rifle, CO 81650
(970) 625-2371

Yampa Ranger District
(Routt NF)
Routt National Forest
300 Roselawn
PO Box 7
Yampa, CO 80483
(970) 638-4516

EMERGENCY SERVICES
All Emergencies - 911

EAGLE COUNTY
Vail Valley Medical Center
181 W. Meadow Drive
Vail, CO 81658
(970) 476-8065

Eagle County Sheriff
0885 E. Chambers Ave.
Avon, CO 81631
(970) 328-8500

GARFIELD COUNTY
Valley View Hospital
1906 Blake Ave.
Glenwood Springs, CO 81601
(970) 945-6535

Clagett Memorial Hospital
701 E 5th
Rifle, CO 81650
(970) 625-1510

Garfield County Sheriff
(970) 945-9151

COLORADO PARKS AND
WILDLIFE
Northwest Region
0088 Wildlife Way
Glenwood Springs, CO 81601
(970) 945-7228

RIO BLANCO COUNTY
Pioneers Hospital
345 Cleveland
Meeker, CO 81641
(970) 878-5047

Rio Blanco County Sheriff
Meeker County Courthouse
555 Main Street
Meeker, CO 81641
(970) 878-5023

Colorado Parks and Wildlife
73485 State Highway 64
Meeker, CO
(970) 878-4493

MOFFAT COUNTY
The Memorial Hospital
785 Russell St.
Craig, CO 81625
(970) 824-9411

Colorado State Patrol
(303) 824-6501

Moffat County Sheriff
911

Routt County
Routt County Hospital
80 Park Ave.
Steamboat Springs, CO 80487
(970) 879-1322

COLORADO STATE PATROL
(303) 879-4306

Routt County Sheriff
911

STATE
Poison Control
(800) 332-3073

COLORADO PARKS AND
WILDLIFE
Central Region
6060 Broadway
Denver, CO 80216
(303) 297-1192

Northwest Region
711 Independent Ave.
Grand Junction, CO 81505
(970) 248-7175

Index

About the Authors

AL MARLOWE has been a fisherman for more than forty years. He has cast a fly or lure into many of the streams and lakes in the Flat Tops Wilderness and the surrounding area. In 1969, he made his first visit to the wilderness to fish Mahaffey Lake. Since that visit he has spent many days fishing and camping in the region.

Al previously taught fly tying and fly fishing classes at Jefferson County Adult Education. He has written articles on fishing and outdoor recreation since 1988. His stories have been published in magazines and on outdoor sports websites. In addition, he has written three books, *A Hiking and Camping Guide to the Flat Tops Wilderness Area*, *Fly Fishing the Colorado River*, and *The Fly Fishing Guide to Colorado's Flat Tops Wilderness*.

KAREN RAE CHRISTOPHERSON has been fishing since her childhood in Boulder, Colorado. A geophysicist by education and training, Karen has traveled extensively throughout the US and across the world, often with her fly rod in tow. Writing has been a passion since school and she feels fortunate to author books about fly fishing as a diversion from the technical world of geosciences. Karen also acts as webmaster for coloradofishing.net and other fishing websites.

Printed in the USA
CPSIA information can be obtained
at www.ICGtesting.com
JSHW012012140824
68134JS00023B/2375